R·E·C·I·P·E·S
for
CANNED
FISH

ACKNOWLEDGEMENTS

The publishers would like to thank the following authors and photographers for the material used in this book: Pat Alburey; June Budgen; Sarah Bush; Per Ericson; Moyra Fraser; Paul Grater; Carole Handslip; Kerenza Harries; Sue Jorgensen; Ken Field; Lesley Mackley; Mary Norwak; James Murphy; Alan Newnham; Lorna Rhodes; Lyn Rutherford; Louise Steele; and Jon Stewart.

Published in 1992 by Merehurst Limited, Ferry House, 51–57 Lacy Road, Putney, London SW15 1PR.

Distributed by J.B. Fairfax Press Limited, 9 Trinity Centre, Park Farm, Wellingborough, Northants NN8 6ZB

ISBN 1–874567–00–X

Edited by Katie Swallow
Designed by Grahame Dudley Associates
Cover photography by James Duncan
Cover food prepared by Joanna Farrow
Cover styling by Madeleine Brehaut

Typeset by J&L Composition Ltd, Station Avenue, Filey, North Yorkshire YO14 9AH.
Colour separation by Fotographics Ltd, UK-Hong Kong
Printed in Italy by New Interlitho S.p.A.

CONTENTS

STARTERS 6

MAIN COURSE DISHES 17

SNACKS & SUPPER DISHES 27

SALADS 41

INDEX 48

NOTES ON USING THE RECIPES

For all recipes, quantities are given in metric and Imperial measurements. Follow one set of measures only as they are not interchangeable. Standard 5ml (tsp) and 15ml (tbsp) are used. Australian readers, whose tablespoons measure 20ml, should adjust quantities accordingly. Ingredients for garnishing and decorating have not been included in ingredient lists. If fresh herbs are not available, substitute 1 teaspoon of dried herbs for every tablespoon of fresh herbs as specified in the recipe.

INTRODUCTION

Canned fish is the ideal food for today's hectic lifestyles. When time is short, what could be quicker than opening a can of fish and assembling a delicious meal in minutes! With the extensive range of canned fish available, from tuna and salmon to mackerel and prawns, everyone's tastes can be catered for. As well as being convenient and tasty, canned fish is also highly nutritious and can play a vital role in a healthy balanced diet.

Canned fish is ready in an instant with no waste or messy preparation. The delicious recipes in this cookbook have been compiled to help you make the most of the wide variety of canned fish available. Whether you want to make something quick and simple like the recipe for Spicy Herrings, or spend a little more time to create something special like the Salmon and Avocado Mousse starter, canned fish is the perfect choice for the busy cook.

Few foods make as valuable a contribution to a healthy diet as canned fish. It is an important source of protein, vital for growth and repair of body cells and tissue. It contains essential vitamins to help fight infection and maintain a normal metabolism and body growth. Canned fish also contains an appreciable quantity of minerals which assist the development of healthy bones and teeth, particularly important for children.

Nowadays we should all be aware of the danger of eating too much saturated fat – the type found in red meats and dairy products for example. The fat present in canned fish, and the oil in which it is packed, is polyunsaturated and considered to be beneficial to health since it does not increase the level of cholesterol in the blood. Research suggests that this may help to prevent heart disease.

And if you are looking to reduce your calorie intake, canned fish in brine is ideal. For example a 125g (4oz) serving of tuna in brine contains only 110 calories compared with tuna in oil which contains 197 calories. There is now an extensive range of canned fish in brine available, not only tuna but also sardines, pilchards, mackerel, shrimps and prawns.

John West canned fish is a natural favourite as only the finest fish are selected before being carefully canned and cooked to ensure that all the flavour and goodness remain safely locked in. And with such a large range of canned fish now available in oil, brine and savoury sauces, together with the exciting recipe ideas in this book, you need never be short of inspiration.

For further information on John West Foods, please write to:

The John West Information Service
PO Box 21
Godalming
Surrey GU7 2SS

SMOKEY MACKEREL MOUSSE

This delicious combination of smoked mackerel, apple, lemon juice and creamy soft cheese is sure to become a firm favourite.

1 small eating apple, cored
15g (½oz) butter
2 × 110g (3¾oz) cans smoked
mackerel, drained
125g (4oz) low-fat soft cheese
grated rind of ½ lemon, plus
1tbsp lemon juice
90g (3oz) thick Greek yogurt
salt and pepper
1tsp powdered gelatine
2 rashers of bacon, rinds
removed
30g (1oz) chopped hazelnuts,
toasted

SERVES FOUR

1 Peel and chop apple. Place in a saucepan with butter and cook for 3 minutes until softened. Set aside to cool.

2 Place apple in food processor with drained mackerel, soft cheese, lemon rind and juice, yogurt and salt and pepper and blend for 1–2 minutes until smooth.

3 Put 2tbsp water in a small bowl. Sprinkle over the gelatine and leave until spongy, then stand bowl in a small pan of hot water and leave for 4–5 minutes until the gelatine is completely dissolved.

4 Add gelatine to fish mixture and blend for a further few seconds.

5 Spoon mixture into a small, deep dish and chill overnight in the refrigerator until set.

6 Grill bacon until very crisp, then crumble. Spoon mousse onto individual serving plates. Sprinkle with bacon and nuts and serve with toasted bread.

VARIATION This mousse can also be made with other canned fish such as white crab, lobster, pilchards or kipper fillets. If liked, add 1tbsp chopped tarragon, parsley, coriander or chervil to the fish mixture at the end of Step 4.

PRAWN & ALMOND SOUP

The smoothness of the almond soup blends unexpectedly well with the prawns.

125g (4oz) white bread, crusts
  removed
250ml (8fl oz) milk
125g (4oz) ground almonds
3tbsp lemon juice
3tbsp olive oil
1 small clove garlic, crushed
60ml (2fl oz) single (light)
  cream
315ml (10fl oz) iced water
salt and pepper
200g (7oz) can prawns, drained

SERVES FOUR

1 Break bread into pieces and put into a bowl. Pour over the milk and leave to soak for 5 minutes.

2 Transfer bread and milk to a food processor and add ground almonds, lemon juice, oil, garlic, cream, water and salt and pepper. Blend until smooth, then transfer to a bowl, cover and chill until required.

3 Spoon soup into individual serving bowls, sprinkle each with prawns and serve.

> SHORTCUT This soup can be prepared the day before it is required and chilled in the refrigerator. Simply add prawns to soup just before serving.

ANCHOVY & PEPPER TWISTS

Cheese pastries twisted with anchovy fillets and red pepper strips.

1 red pepper
125g (4oz) plain flour, sifted
pinch of salt
pinch of cayenne pepper
¼tsp mustard powder
60g (2oz) Cheddar cheese,
  grated
90g (3oz) butter
3 egg yolks
3 × 50g (1¾oz) cans anchovies,
  drained
1 egg white, lightly beaten

MAKES APPROXIMATELY SEVENTY

1 Preheat oven to 200°C (400°F/Gas 6). Cook red pepper under a hot grill, turning frequently, until skin wrinkles and scorches slightly. Cool, then skin and remove seeds. Cut flesh into strips 5mm (¼in) wide and 10cm (4in) long.

2 Put flour, salt, cayenne pepper and mustard into a bowl, then mix in cheese. Rub in butter until mixture resembles fine breadcrumbs. Add egg yolks and 2tsp water; mix to a dough.

3 Roll dough out on a floured surface to an oblong 32.5 × 22.5cm (13 × 9in). Trim. Cut in half lengthwise. Cutting across halves, cut into thin strips about 5mm (¼in) wide.

4 Halve anchovy fillets lengthwise. Take a pastry strip and pepper strip and twist together. Place on greased baking sheet. Repeat with remaining pepper and anchovies to make 70. Brush with egg white. Bake for 10–15 minutes. Cool.

SALMON & AVOCADO MOUSSE

This impressive-looking salmon and avocado mousse is surprisingly easy
to prepare and makes a perfect dinner party starter.

1 quantity of Salmon Mousse,
see below, omitting
cucumber
2 avocados
2tbsp lemon juice
2tsp salt
2tbsp gelatine
250ml (8fl oz) boiling water
1tbsp single (light) cream

SERVES SIX

1 Pour prepared salmon mousse into a 750ml (24fl oz) tin lined with plastic wrap. Chill until beginning to set around edges.

2 Halve, stone and remove flesh from avocados. Blend in a food processor with lemon juice and salt until smooth.

3 Dissolve gelatine in boiling water and add to avocado. Blend until smooth, then add cream. Put into a large piping bag fitted with a plain tube.

4 Hold nozzle of piping bag below surface of the Salmon Mousse and pipe in the avocado mixture, at the same time running the nozzle along to the end of the loaf tin.

5 Chill mousse until set. Remove from tin and serve sliced.

SALMON MOUSSE

A creamy salmon and cucumber mousse flavoured with mustard
and paprika.

1 cucumber
418g (14oz) can red salmon,
drained
1tbsp gelatine
125ml (4fl oz) boiling water
½tsp dry mustard
2tbsp white wine vinegar
1tsp paprika
250ml (8fl oz) single (light)
cream

SERVES FOUR

1 Trim cucumber ends and cut lengthwise into thin slices. Line a long narrow 500ml (16fl oz) loaf tin with slices.

2 Blend salmon in a food processor. Dissolve gelatine in the boiling water and pour over the salmon. Add mustard, vinegar and paprika and blend until smooth.

3 Add cream and blend until just mixed. Pour into lined tin and chill until set. Turn out of mould, cut into slices and serve.

VARIATION If preferred replace mustard and paprika with 1tbsp chopped fresh dill or 1tsp dried. Serve with slices of toasted brown bread, or melba toast and garnish with lemon or lime slices.

TUNA & BASIL TOMATOES

Tomatoes filled with a tuna and basil soufflé mixture and served on slices of crispy bread.

4 medium beef tomatoes
salt and pepper
four 2.5cm (1in) thick slices
  white bread, crusts removed
90g (3oz) butter
1 garlic clove, crushed
1tbsp chopped parsley
185g (6oz) tuna chunks in
  brine, drained
1tsp pesto sauce
1 egg, separated
1tsp grated Parmesan cheese

SERVES FOUR

1 Preheat oven to 200°C (400°F/Gas 6). Cut tops off tomatoes and hollow out with a teaspoon. Season insides of tomatoes; turn upside down to drain.

2 Using a 5cm (2in) pastry cutter, cut a hole in centre of each slice of bread. Make breadcrumbs with cut out pieces and reserve.

3 Melt 60g (2oz) butter with garlic. Add parsley and brush over both sides of each slice of bread, then put onto a baking sheet.

4 Melt remaining butter and stir in tuna, 2tbsp reserved breadcrumbs and pesto sauce. Whisk egg white until stiff. Stir egg yolk into tuna and fold in egg white.

5 Place tomatoes in holes in bread and fill with tuna mixture. Top with cheese and bake for 12–15 minutes until soufflé is risen and golden and bread is crisp.

ANCHOVY BEIGNETS

Serve these delicious morsels on a bed of salad leaves for an unusual starter.

60g (2oz) butter, cubed
60g (2oz) plain flour
4 canned anchovy fillets,
    drained and mashed
2 eggs
30g (1oz) flaked almonds
vegetable oil for deep-frying

SERVES FOUR

1 Place butter in a saucepan with 125ml (4fl oz) water; heat until butter melts, then bring butter and water mixture to the boil.

2 Add flour all at once and stir for about 1 minute, until paste leaves sides of pan. Cool. Transfer to a bowl. Beat in anchovy fillets and eggs, one at a time, until mixture is glossy. Stir in almonds.

3 Heat oil in a pan. When hot, drop a few teaspoonfuls of the mixture into the oil. Cook a few at a time for about 5 minutes until golden. Remove and drain on absorbent kitchen paper. Repeat until all batter is used. Serve hot.

> **VARIATION** If preferred replace almonds with chopped mixed nuts or pine nuts and stir in 1tsp dried mixed herbs in Step 2.

KIPPER & LEMON PATE

Kipper pâté served in hollowed-out lemon shells makes an impressive dinner party starter.

4 medium lemons
190g (6oz) can kipper fillets in vegetable oil, drained
90g (3oz) low-fat soft cheese
1tsp horseradish sauce
1tbsp lemon juice
30g (1oz) wholemeal breadcrumbs
1tbsp chopped chives

SERVES FOUR

1 With the point of a serrated knife edge, cut round the top third of the lemons in a zig-zag style and remove lids.

2 Scoop the flesh out and press through a sieve to extract the juice. Remove any pith inside the lemon shells.

3 Place kippers in a food processor with soft cheese, horseradish sauce and lemon juice and blend to a rough paste. Turn into a bowl and stir in breadcrumbs and chives.

4 Divide mixture between lemon shells. Serve with melba toast.

> **VARIATION** Replace low-fat soft cheese with other flavoured soft cheeses of your choice such as garlic and herb or peppercorn.

ANCHOVY TOASTS

Soaking anchovies in milk helps to reduce some of their saltiness.

50g (1¾oz) can anchovies, drained
1tbsp milk
30g (1oz) butter, softened
30g (1oz) cream cheese
1tsp lemon juice
large pinch each of cayenne pepper and ground nutmeg
¼tsp Tabasco sauce
2tsp capers, drained and finely chopped
fingers of hot toast

SERVES FOUR

1 Put anchovies in a bowl with milk. Soak for 30 minutes. Drain well and pat dry with absorbent kitchen paper.

2 Chop anchovies finely and put into a bowl with the butter and cream cheese. Mix well, then add lemon juice, cayenne, nutmeg and Tabasco sauce.

3 Place mixture in a food processor and blend until smooth. Stir in capers. Serve with hot toast.

> **VARIATION** This anchovy spread is ideal party food: Serve spread on different shapes of bread such as stars, triangles and squares. Try serving with different types of bread too. This spread will keep, covered, in the refrigerator for up to 5 days.

15

TUNA & PRAWN PATE

This quick and easy pâté of tuna and prawns makes a good starter for midweek meals. Serve with crackers or Melba toast.

30g (1oz) butter
6 spring onions, chopped
1 clove garlic, crushed
400g (13oz) can tuna chunks in
  brine, drained
4tbsp single (light) cream
100g (3½oz) can prawns,
  drained
1tbsp lemon juice
good pinch of cayenne pepper
salt and pepper

SERVES FOUR

1 Melt butter in a saucepan and sauté spring onions and garlic for 2 minutes until softened. Set aside to cool.

2 Place onion mixture, tuna and cream in a food processor and blend until smooth. Add prawns, lemon juice, cayenne pepper and salt and pepper, and blend for a few seconds.

3 Transfer mixture to 4 small dishes, cover and chill until firm.

SEAFOOD LASAGNE

Ring the changes with this delicious mackerel and prawn lasagne.

90g (3oz) butter
4 carrots, finely chopped
1 onion, chopped
3 sticks celery, finely chopped
60g (2oz) plain flour
470ml (15fl oz) milk
90g (3oz) Cheddar cheese,
  grated
2 × 200g (6½oz) cans mackerel
  steak in brine, drained
  and flaked
100g (3½oz) can prawns,
  drained
1tbsp chopped parsley
pinch of grated nutmeg
salt and pepper
6 sheets oven-ready lasagne
30g (1oz) grated Parmesan
  cheese

SERVES FOUR

1 Preheat oven to 190°C (375°F/Gas 5). Melt 30g (1oz) butter in a saucepan and sauté carrots, onion and celery for 5 minutes until softened.

2 Melt remaining butter in another pan. Stir in flour, remove from heat and gradually add milk. Return pan to heat and bring to the boil, stirring.

3 Remove pan from heat and add carrot mixture, Cheddar cheese, mackerel, prawns, parsley, nutmeg and salt and pepper.

4 Arrange a layer of lasagne in base of a buttered ovenproof dish. Cover with one third of fish sauce. Repeat layers twice, ending with sauce. Sprinkle with Parmesan cheese and bake for 25–30 minutes.

> SHORTCUT Prepare dish up to a day in advance and keep covered in refrigerator until ready to cook.

MIDWEEK PILCHARD BAKE

Prepare this delicious bake in advance if liked and store in refrigerator until ready to bake.

425g (15oz) can pilchards in brine, drained
1tbsp mustard powder
315ml (10fl oz) natural yogurt
4 courgettes, thinly sliced
4 tomatoes, thinly sliced
2 onions, chopped
60g (2oz) Cheddar cheese, grated

SERVES FOUR

1 Preheat oven to 180°C (350°F/Gas 4). Fork pilchards roughly with mustard and blend in yogurt. Put half the pilchard mixture in an ovenproof dish.

2 Arrange courgettes, tomatoes and onions on top of the pilchards, then cover with remaining fish mixture. Sprinkle with cheese and bake for 30 minutes until golden.

> **VARIATION** Replace pilchards with herring fillets in savoury sauce, mackerel fillets in brine or tuna in sweet and sour sauce.

FISHERMAN'S PIE

Tuna and vegetables topped with crispy potato slices.

750g (1½lb) medium potatoes
salt and pepper
45g (1½oz) butter
1 small onion, finely chopped
30g (1oz) plain flour
400g (13oz) can tuna chunks in brine
155ml (5fl oz) milk
250g (8oz) frozen mixed vegetables

SERVES FOUR

1 Preheat oven to 200°C (400°F/Gas 6). Peel potatoes and place in a saucepan of salted water. Boil for 7–8 minutes until tender.

2 Meanwhile, melt 30g (1oz) butter in a pan, add onion and cook for 3 minutes until softened. Stir in flour.

3 Drain fish and make liquid up to 315ml (10fl oz) with milk. Gradually add milk to onion, then bring to the boil and cook until thickened, stirring. Add tuna, vegetables and salt and pepper.

4 Pour fish mixture into an ovenproof dish. Drain potatoes and cut into 5mm (¼in) slices. Arrange potato over tuna. Melt remaining butter and brush over the potatoes. Bake for 20–25 minutes until golden. Serve with a mixed salad.

> **SHORTCUT** Keep the freezer stocked with a good selection of vegetables ready to prepare this simple, but delicious supper dish.

18

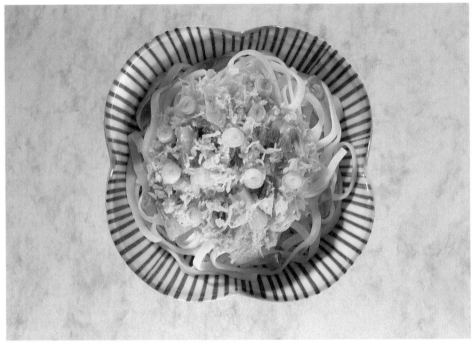

CRAB MEAT & NOODLES

250g (8oz) egg noodles
salt
2tbsp vegetable oil
250g (8oz) Chinese leaves,
  roughly shredded
170g (5½oz) can white crab
  meat, drained
3-4tsp Tabasco sauce
2tsp soy sauce
250ml (8fl oz) light stock
2 spring onions, finely
  chopped

SERVES FOUR

1 Cook noodles in a large saucepan of boiling salted water until just tender. Drain well. Put into a hot serving dish and keep warm.

2 Heat oil in a large frying pan or wok and stir-fry Chinese leaves for 2 minutes. Add crab, Tabasco sauce, soy sauce and stock and cook for 3–4 minutes.

3 Pour sauce over noodles. Sprinkle with spring onions and serve.

> **VARIATION** If Chinese leaves are not available, replace with fresh beansprouts and add to frying pan or wok with crab meat.

TUNA BAKE

Serve this tasty supper dish with crusty French bread and a mixed salad.

60g (2oz) small pasta shells
salt
200g (7oz) can tuna steak in
  oil, drained
1tsp French mustard
2tsp Worcestershire sauce
juice ½ lemon
125ml (4fl oz) natural yogurt
cayenne pepper
6tsp fresh breadcrumbs
30g (1oz) grated Parmesan
  cheese

SERVES TWO

1 Cook pasta in a saucepan of boiling salted water for 3-4 minutes until tender. Drain.

2 Combine tuna, mustard, Worcestershire sauce, lemon juice, yoghurt and pasta. Season with salt and cayenne pepper.

3 Spoon fish mixture into 2 individual heatproof dishes and top with breadcrumbs and Parmesan cheese. Place dishes under a medium grill and cook for about 10 minutes until golden.

> **VARIATION** Replace tuna with crab meat if wished. This dish makes a good starter for 6: Divide mixture between 6 small heatproof dishes and continue recipe as above.

SARDINE COBBLER

Topped with miniature fish-shaped scones, the children will love this quick and easy supper dish.

2tbsp vegetable oil
1 leek, sliced
60g (2oz) button mushrooms, sliced
2 × 120g (4oz) cans sardines in tomato sauce

TOPPING
60g (2oz) margarine
250g (8oz) self-raising flour
1tbsp rolled oats
250ml (8fl oz) milk

SERVES FOUR

1 Preheat oven to 200°C (400°F/Gas 6). Heat oil in a saucepan, add leeks and mushrooms and sauté for 3 minutes until just tender.

2 Place vegetables in a shallow ovenproof dish. Add sardines and 4tbsp water.

3 Rub margarine into flour, add rolled oats and bind to a pliable dough with the milk. Roll dough to a 1cm (½in) thickness on a lightly floured surface and stamp out 20 fish shapes using a 5cm (2in) fish-shaped cutter.

4 Arrange fish shapes on top of sardines. Bake for 20–25 minutes until golden.

> **VARIATION** Replace sardines with herrings in savoury sauce or pilchards in tomato sauce if preferred.

SAVOURY CRUMBLE

Mackerel combined with cauliflower and celery and topped with a cheesy crumble.

125g (4oz) cauliflower florets
2 sticks celery, cut into 2.5cm (1in) lengths
pinch of salt
125g (4oz) can mackerel fillets in tomato sauce
1tbsp milk

TOPPING
30g (1oz) margarine
60g (2oz) plain flour
30g (1oz) Cheddar cheese, grated

SERVES FOUR

1 Preheat oven to 200°C (400°F/Gas 6). Put cauliflower and celery in a saucepan, add salt, cover with boiling water and cook for 10–15 minutes until just tender. Drain well.

2 Put vegetables in an ovenproof dish with mackerel. Mix some of the tomato sauce from the fish with the milk and pour over mackerel.

3 For topping, rub margarine into flour until it resembles breadcrumbs, then add cheese. Spread topping over fish mixture and bake for 15–20 minutes until golden.

> **SHORTCUT** Make up a large batch of topping mixture and freeze in individual bags for up to 3 months for quick and easy last minute midweek suppers.

TUNA & MACARONI LAYER

Tuna, wholewheat macaroni and chopped egg in a lemon and parsley sauce.

185g (6oz) wholewheat
  macaroni
salt and pepper
90g (3oz) Cheddar cheese,
  grated
30g (1oz) butter
30g (1oz) plain flour
155ml (5fl oz) milk
200g (7oz) can tuna in oil,
  drained
2tsp lemon juice
2 hard-boiled eggs, chopped
1tbsp chopped parsley

SERVES FOUR

1   Cook macaroni in a large saucepan of boiling salted water for 5–6 minutes until tender. Drain and mix with 60g (2oz) cheese.

2   Melt butter in a pan, stir in flour and cook for 1 minute. Remove from heat and gradually blend in milk. Return to heat and cook until thickened, stirring. Remove from heat.

3   Flake tuna into white sauce. Stir in lemon juice, eggs, parsley and salt and pepper. Cook for 1–2 minutes until warmed through.

4   Divide tuna between 4 individual heatproof dishes. Top with macaroni and remaining cheese. Grill until golden.

ANCHOVY & PEPPER GRATIN

An unusual supper dish of spaghetti layered with anchovies and mixed peppers.

2 large red peppers, halved and seeded
2 large yellow peppers, halved and seeded
125ml (4fl oz) olive oil
1 clove garlic, crushed
4 canned anchovies, drained and chopped
8 black olives, stoned and chopped
3tsp capers
salt and pepper
250g (8oz) spaghetti
2tbsp fresh breadcrumbs
2tbsp grated Parmesan cheese

SERVES FOUR

1 Preheat oven to 190°C (375°F/Gas 5). Cook peppers under a hot grill until skins are blistered and scorched. Cool, then remove skins. Cut peppers into strips.

2 Heat half the oil in a frying pan. Add peppers and garlic and sauté for 2–3 minutes. Stir in anchovies, olives, capers and salt and pepper.

3 Meanwhile cook spaghetti in a large pan of boiling salted water until tender. Drain, return to pan; toss in half remaining olive oil.

4 Mix breadcrumbs and Parmesan cheese and sprinkle half over base of ovenproof dish. Top with half the peppers, then with spaghetti. Cover with remaining peppers. Top with remaining crumbs and cheese. Pour over remaining oil.

5 Bake for 20 minutes until golden and crisp.

SPICY HERRINGS

Herring fillets cooked in a delicious spicy ginger and lemon sauce.

1tbsp vegetable oil
1 onion, sliced
large pinch ground ginger
pinch of garlic salt
1tbsp soy sauce
1tsp sugar
juice ½ lemon
2 × 190g (7oz) cans herring
*   fillets in tomato sauce*

SERVES FOUR

1   Heat oil in a frying pan, add onion and sauté for 3 minutes until softened. Add ginger and garlic salt and cook for 1 minute.

2   Stir soy sauce, sugar and lemon juice into pan. Add herring fillets. Rinse out the can with 4tbsp water and pour over the fish. Heat through for 5–10 minutes, then serve with boiled rice.

> **VARIATION** Serve this dish with a selection of stir-fried vegetables such as mange tout, beansprouts or shredded cabbage flavoured with soy sauce.

BASIC CREPES

125g (4oz) plain flour, sifted
pinch of salt
2 eggs
315ml (10fl oz) milk
15g (½oz) butter, melted
vegetable oil for cooking

MAKES EIGHT

1   Place flour and salt in a bowl. Make a well in centre and add eggs and a little milk. Beat in remaining milk and butter.

2   Heat a little vegetable oil in an 18cm (7in) crêpe pan, barely covering the base. Pour in 2–3tbsp batter, tilting pan so batter covers the base thinly and evenly. Cook over a high heat for 1 minute until lightly brown underneath.

3   Turn crêpe with a palette knife and cook other side for 30 seconds. Remove from pan and keep warm. Repeat with remaining batter.

> **VARIATION**   For wholemeal crêpes, replace flour with plain wholemeal flour. Use 3 eggs instead of 2 and omit melted butter.

TRADITIONAL PIZZA DOUGH

345g (11oz) strong white flour, sifted
1 heaped tsp salt
15g (½oz) fresh yeast; or 1tsp dried active yeast and 1tsp sugar; or 1tsp easy blend yeast
185ml (6fl oz) hand-hot water
1tbsp olive oil

1   Put flour and salt into a large bowl.

2   In a small bowl, mix fresh yeast with a little of the water; put in a warm place until frothy. To use dried active yeast, mix with sugar and a little water; leave until frothy. (To use easy blend yeast, mix into flour and salt before adding water and oil.) Add yeast to flour with remaining water and oil and mix to a dough; knead 10 minutes. Put in a greased bowl, cover and put in a warm place for 45 minutes until doubled in size.

3   Knock back dough and knead. Press dough into an oiled 30cm (12in) pizza tin. Pinch up edges. Use as recipe instructs.

DEEP PAN PIZZA DOUGH

155g (5oz) strong white flour, sifted
155g (5oz) plain flour, sifted
1 heaped tsp salt
15g (½oz) fresh yeast; or 1tsp dried active yeast and 1tsp sugar; or 1tsp easy blend yeast
185ml (6fl oz) hand-hot water
1tbsp olive oil

1   Make dough as for Traditional Pizza Dough. When dough has doubled in size, knock back and knead briefly.

2   Press dough into an oiled 25cm (10in) deep sandwich tin. Cover and put in a warm place for 1½ hours until risen almost to top of tin. Use as recipe instructs.

ORIENTAL OMELETTE

Prawns, waterchestnuts and fresh coriander make a delicious filling for
this Oriental-inspired omelette.

4 eggs
15–30g (1–2oz) butter

FILLING
2tbsp vegetable oil
1 clove garlic, crushed
1 carrot, cut into thin strips
2 spring onions, sliced
90g (3oz) mange tout (snow peas), topped and tailed
6 water chestnuts, chopped
100g (3½oz) can prawns, drained
handful of coriander leaves
2tsp light soy sauce

SERVES TWO

1 For filling, heat oil in a frying pan. Add garlic, carrot, spring onion and stir-fry for 2 minutes. Add mange tout and cook for 1 minute. Stir in remaining ingredients and heat through. Transfer to bowl and keep hot.

2 For omelette, beat eggs with 4tbsp water. Melt half the butter in a frying pan and pour in half of the egg mixture. As edges of omelette set, push them towards the centre, allowing runny mixture to fill the pan. Continue cooking in this way until omelette is set. Transfer to warmed plate, and repeat with remaining ingredients.

3 Divide filling between omelettes and serve immediately.

PRAWN & PEPPER CREPES

Crêpes with a prawn and nut filling served with a tomato and red
pepper sauce.

8 × 18cm (7in) Basic Crêpes, see page 27
30g (1oz) butter

SAUCE
1 red pepper, halved and seeded
3 tomatoes
1 clove garlic, unpeeled
2tbsp olive oil

FILLING
30g (1oz) chopped mixed nuts
30g (1oz) butter
1 clove garlic, crushed
2tbsp chopped parsley
500g (1lb) spinach
200g (7oz) can prawns, drained
2tsp lemon juice
salt and pepper

SERVES FOUR

1 For sauce, grill peppers, skin-side up, for 10–12 minutes until skin is browned. After 5 minutes, add tomatoes and garlic and cook in same way for 5–7 minutes. Peel away skins of vegetables and garlic, then blend in food processor with oil until smooth. Set aside.

2 For filling, preheat oven to 190°C (375°F/Gas 5). Brown nuts in a saucepan, stirring constantly; remove. Add butter to pan with garlic and parsley and cook for 1 minute. Add spinach and cook for 2–3 minutes until just wilted, stirring. Squeeze out excess moisture, then add nuts, prawns, lemon juice and salt and pepper.

3 Divide filling between crêpes and fold to enclose. Use some of butter to grease an ovenproof dish and arrange crêpes in dish in one layer. Dot with remaining butter, cover and bake for 20 minutes. Serve with hot pepper sauce.

28

CHEESY ANCHOVY CREPES

Anchovies and Gruyère cheese combined in a thick soured cream sauce.

8 × 18cm (7in) Wholemeal Crêpes, see page 27

FILLING
2 × 50g (1¾oz) cans anchovies, drained and finely chopped
125g (4oz) Gruyère cheese, cut into thin strips
155ml (5fl oz) thick soured cream
1tbsp lemon juice
pepper

SERVES FOUR

1 Keep crêpes warm while preparing filling.

2 Mix anchovies, cheese, soured cream, lemon juice and pepper together.

3 Divide filling between crêpes and roll up. Serve at once.

> **VARIATION** If preferred the cheese and soured cream sauce can be served warm. Simply heat through in a saucepan, taking care not to let the sauce boil.

PRAWN & TUNA CREPES

Prawns and tuna in a light and creamy green pepper sauce.

8 × 18cm (7in) Basic Crêpes, see page 27

FILLING
45g (1½oz) butter
1 small green pepper, seeded and finely chopped
15g (½oz) plain flour
155ml (5fl oz) chicken stock
100g (3½oz) can prawns, drained
200g (7oz) can tuna steak in brine, drained and flaked
155ml (5fl oz) single (light) cream
salt and pepper

SERVES FOUR

1 Preheat oven to 180°C (350°F/Gas 4). Keep crêpes warm while preparing filling.

2 Melt butter in a saucepan and cook green pepper for 3 minutes until softened. Add flour and cook for 1 minute, stirring well.

3 Stir in chicken stock and simmer until thick, stirring constantly. Stir in prawns, tuna, cream and salt and pepper and heat through. Do not boil.

4 Divide mixture between crêpes. Roll up and put in a single layer in an ovenproof dish. Cover with foil and bake for 15 minutes.

MACKEREL & TOMATO CREPES

8 × 18cm (7in) Basic Crêpes,
see page 27

FILLING
30g (1oz) butter
30g (1oz) plain flour
250ml (8fl oz) milk
200g (6½oz) can mackerel steak
in brine, drained
4 tomatoes, skinned, seeded
and chopped
1tbsp lemon juice
salt and pepper
90g (3oz) Cheddar cheese,
grated

SERVES FOUR

1 Keep crêpes warm while preparing filling. Preheat oven to 190°C (375°F/Gas 5).

2 Melt butter in a saucepan, stir in flour and cook for 30 seconds. Remove pan from heat and gradually stir in milk. Return to heat and cook until sauce is thick and smooth, stirring constantly.

3 Remove pan from heat. Stir mackerel, tomatoes, lemon juice and salt and pepper into half the sauce. Divide fish mixture between crêpes and roll up.

4 Put crêpes in a single layer in a shallow ovenproof dish. Stir cheese into remaining sauce and spoon over crêpes. Bake for 20 minutes until golden.

> SHORTCUT Make up several batches of basic crêpes. When cold, stack with interleaving sheets of greaseproof paper, then wrap tightly in foil. Label and freeze for up to 6 months. Thaw then fill as above.

MACKEREL & EGG CREPES

8 × 18cm (7in) Basic Crêpes,
see page 27

FILLING
30g (1oz) butter
30g (1oz) plain flour
250ml (8fl oz) milk
200g (6½oz) can mackerel steak
in brine, drained
1tbsp lemon juice
2 hard-boiled eggs, chopped
2tsp chopped dill
30g (1oz) grated Parmesan
cheese

SERVES FOUR

1 Keep crêpes warm while preparing filling.

2 Melt butter in a saucepan, stir in flour and cook for 30 seconds. Remove from heat and stir in milk. Return to heat and cook until sauce is thick and smooth, stirring constantly.

3 Remove from heat and stir in mackerel, lemon juice, eggs and dill.

4 Divide mixture between crêpes. Roll up and arrange in a single layer in a shallow flameproof serving dish. Top with cheese and place under a hot grill for 2 minutes until golden.

SEAFOOD CREPES

Crêpes topped with a cheesy crab and prawn sauce.

8 × 18cm (7in) Basic Crêpes,
  see page 27

TOPPING
30g (1oz) butter
1 small red pepper, seeded and
  finely chopped
30g (1oz) plain flour
250ml (8fl oz) milk
60g (2oz) Cheddar cheese,
  grated
170g (5½oz) can white crab
  meat, drained
200g (7oz) can prawns, drained
½tsp mustard powder
salt and pepper

SERVES FOUR

1 Keep crêpes warm while preparing topping. Melt butter in a saucepan, add red pepper and cook for 3 minutes until softened. Stir in flour and cook for 1 minute, stirring.

2 Remove pan from heat and gradually stir in milk. Return to heat and bring to boil until sauce is thick and smooth, stirring constantly.

3 Stir in cheese, crab meat, prawns, mustard and salt and pepper and heat through gently. Spoon over crêpes and serve.

DEVILLED CRAB QUICHE

PASTRY

250g (8oz) plain flour, sifted
½tsp salt
½tsp chilli powder
60g (2oz) block margarine, diced
60g (2oz) white vegetable fat, diced
60g (2oz) Cheddar cheese, grated

FILLING

6 streaky bacon rashers, chopped
1 onion, chopped
95g (3oz) can white crab meat, drained
3 eggs
90ml (3fl oz) milk
60ml (2fl oz) single (light) cream
½tsp dry mustard
¼tsp cayenne pepper

SERVES SIX

1 Preheat oven to 200°C (400°F/Gas 6). Put flour, salt and chilli powder into a bowl. Rub in margarine and lard until mixture resembles breadcrumbs. Stir in cheese. Stir in 3tbsp cold water and mix to form a firm dough. Knead gently.

2 Roll out pastry on a lightly floured surface and line a 25cm (10in) loose-bottomed flan tin. Prick base with fork. Line tin with piece of greaseproof paper and fill with baking beans.

3 Bake for 15 minutes, then remove paper and beans. Return flan to oven for 5–10 minutes until golden.

4 Dry-fry bacon in a saucepan for 3 minutes. Add onion and cook for 2 minutes. Remove from heat and add flaked crab meat. Spoon mixture into flan case. Whisk eggs, milk, cream, mustard and cayenne pepper together. Pour into flan case and bake for 30–35 minutes until set and golden.

ALL RECIPES SERVE TWO. CLOCKWISE FROM TOP

TUNA & HORSERADISH SANDWICHES

100g (3½oz) can tuna in oil
1tsp horseradish sauce
2 thick slices wholemeal
  French bread
1tbsp snipped chives

Mash undrained tuna with horseradish sauce.
Spread mixture over bread and top with chives.

SPICY PILCHARD TREATS

230g (7½oz) can pilchards in
  tomato sauce
1tsp curry powder
2 thick slices seeded
  wholemeal bread
2 cherry tomatoes, sliced

Mash undrained pilchards with curry powder.
Spread mixture over bread and top with tomato.

SILD & GHERKIN SLICES

110g (3¾oz) can sild in oil,
  drained
2tbsp sliced gherkins
2 thin slices brown bread,
  buttered
8 black olives

Arrange sild with gherkins over buttered bread
slices. Cut each slice diagonally in half and top each
half with 2 black olives.

SALMON SALAD POCKETS

2 pitta bread
105g (3¾oz) can pink salmon
1tbsp fruit chutney
1tsp tomato purée (paste)
2 lettuce leaves
1 tomato, sliced

Warm pitta bread under grill. Cut a slit in each and
open out the pocket. Mash undrained salmon with
chutney and tomato paste. Fill pitta pockets with
lettuce, tomato and salmon mixture.

CHEESY SARDINE SNACKS

120g (4oz) can sardines in
  tomato sauce
60g (2oz) Cheddar cheese,
  grated
2 thick slices wholemeal
  French bread
few parsley sprigs

Mash undrained sardines with cheese. Spread
mixture over bread slices and top with parsley.

SKIPPER POACHIES

106g (3¾oz) can skippers in
  oil, drained
2 thick slices seeded
  wholemeal bread
2 eggs

Arrange skippers on bread slices. Put under a
moderate grill to heat through. Meanwhile, poach
eggs according to taste. Place eggs on top of
skippers and serve.

TUNA & ONION PIZZA

Tuna, tomatoes and spring onions make a popular pizza topping.

1 quantity of Deep Pan Pizza Dough, shaped and ready for topping, see page 27

TOPPING
2tbsp vegetable oil
440g (14oz) can chopped tomatoes
1 bunch spring onions, chopped
200g (7oz) can tuna steak in oil, drained
salt and pepper

SERVES SIX

1 Preheat oven to 220°C (425°F/Gas 7). Brush pizza dough with 1tbsp oil. Bake for 20 minutes until golden and well risen.

2 For topping, heat remaining oil and tomatoes in a saucepan. Add half the spring onions to pan and cook for 10 minutes. Flake tuna, and stir into tomato mixture with salt and pepper.

3 Spoon fish mixture onto dough and bake for 3–5 minutes. Shred remaining spring onions and sprinkle over pizza.

> VARIATION This pizza is equally as delicious made with sardines in tomato sauce. Storecupboard ingredients such as canned sweetcorn, unsalted nuts and olives also make tasty additions.

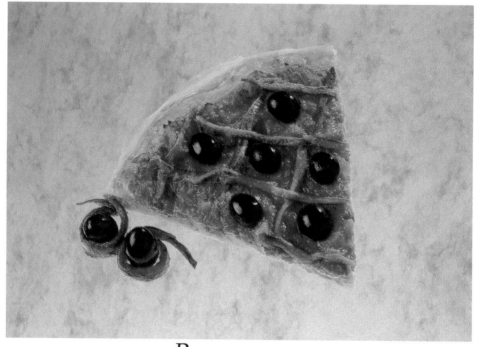

PISSALADIERE

A classic pizza of onions, tomatoes, anchovies and cheese.

*1 quantity of Traditional Pizza
Dough, shaped and ready
for topping, see page 27*

TOPPING
*440g (14oz) can crushed
tomatoes*
1 onion, chopped
1 clove garlic, crushed
2tbsp olive oil
1tbsp chopped parsley
2tsp chopped thyme
1tbsp tomato purée (paste)
1 egg
*60g (2oz) Gruyère cheese,
grated*
salt and pepper
*2 × 50g (1¾oz) cans anchovies,
drained and cut into strips*
15 black olives, halved

SERVES FOUR

1 Preheat oven to 200°C (400°F/Gas 6).

2 For topping, heat tomatoes, onion, garlic, 1tbsp oil, parsley, thyme and tomato paste together. Bring to boil, then simmer for 30 minutes. Cool slightly.

3 Brush dough with remaining oil. Beat egg and stir into tomato mixture with cheese and salt and pepper. Spread over dough. Arrange anchovies in a lattice over pizza. Add black olives and bake for 20 minutes until dough is crisp and golden.

> **VARIATION** For a herb or nut pizza base, knead 2tbsp chopped herbs or 30g (1oz) chopped nuts into pizza dough.

39

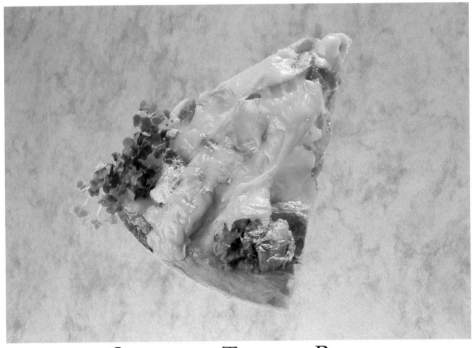

SARDINE & TOMATO PIZZA

Sardines, tomatoes and cheese make a delicous pizza topping.

1 quantity of Traditional Pizza Dough, shaped and ready for topping, see page 27

TOPPING
120g (4oz) can sardines in tomato sauce
2 tomatoes, sliced
125g (4oz) Cheddar cheese, sliced

SERVES SIX

1 Preheat oven to 220°C (425°F/Gas 7). Split sardines horizontally in half and arrange around edge of pizza base. Spoon over tomato sauce from can.

2 Make a circle of overlapping tomatoes in centre of pizza. Cut cheese into strips and arrange over tomatoes. Bake for 20 minutes until dough is crisp and golden.

SHORTCUT If liked, prepare pizza dough a day before it is needed and allow to prove in an airtight bag in the refrigerator overnight. Assemble with topping ingredients just before baking.

SMOKED MACKEREL SALAD

New potatoes, smoked mackerel and cucumber in a mustard dressing.

500g (1lb) new potatoes
2 × 110g (3¾oz) cans smoked
  mackerel, drained
¼ cucumber, peeled and
  chopped

DRESSING
3tbsp sunflower oil
1tbsp wholegrain mustard
1tbsp lemon juice

SERVES FOUR

1 Cook potatoes in their skins in a large saucepan of boiling water for 8–10 minutes until tender. Drain. When cool enough to handle, remove skins if liked, and quarter.

2 Flake mackerel into a bowl. Add potatoes and cucumber.

3 Mix dressing ingredients together, then stir into mackerel salad.

> **SHORTCUT** When preparing potatoes for the family meal, cook extra for this salad so it can be assembled in next-to-no-time the following day.

CRAB & MACKEREL SALAD

Serve this crab and mackerel salad with crusty brown bread or melba toast as a main course dish or as part of a buffet table.

170g (5½oz) can white crab meat, drained
110g (3¾oz) can smoked mackerel, drained
2tbsp mayonnaise
1tbsp single (light) cream
2tbsp lemon juice
salt and pepper
125g (4oz) salad leaves, eg red oakleaf, endive, roquette, corn lettuce
1 box mustard and cress
small handful of snipped chives
8 cherry tomatoes, halved

DRESSING
2tbsp olive oil
2tsp white wine vinegar
½tsp grated lemon rind
pinch of sugar
salt and pepper

SERVES FOUR

1 Place crab meat and mackerel in a bowl. Stir in mayonnaise, cream, lemon juice and salt and pepper.

2 Place salad leaves, mustard and cress, herbs and tomatoes in a separate bowl.

3 Stir dressing ingredients together, then pour over leafy salad and toss gently to mix. Divide between individual serving plates and top with fish mixture.

VARIATION Other combinations of canned fish can be used in this salad. Try salmon and prawn; crab and smoked mussels; or tuna and baby clams. Replace chives with other herbs of your choice such as parsley, tarragon, or dill, or a mixture. Add 1tsp horseradish relish or a few drops of Tabasco sauce to the dressing if preferred.

42

PASTA & PRAWN SALAD

Pasta, prawns and smoked salmon in a parsley and tarragon dressing.

250g (8oz) mixed pasta shells
salt and pepper
200g (7oz) can prawns, drained
125g (4oz) smoked salmon,
cut into strips

DRESSING
3tbsp olive oil
1tbsp lemon juice
1tbsp tomato juice
1tbsp chopped parsley
1tbsp chopped tarragon
salt and pepper

SERVES FOUR

1 Cook pasta in a saucepan of boiling salted water for 6-8 minutes until just tender. Drain, rinse under cold water and drain again.

2 Put pasta into a bowl with prawns and salmon.

3 Mix dressing ingredients and salt and pepper together in a bowl. Pour dressing over salad, then transfer to serving dish.

VARIATION For midweek suppers, replace salmon with flaked tuna or sardines; or Cheddar or Emmenthal cheese.

44

CRAB & AVOCADO SALAD

Crab and avocado in a creamy tomato and mayonnaise sauce.

2 avocados
1tbsp lemon juice
2 × 170g (5½oz) cans white
crab meat, drained and
flaked

SAUCE
60ml (2fl oz) mayonnaise
½tsp Worcestershire sauce
60ml (2fl oz) single (light)
cream
2tsp lemon juice
1tsp dry sherry
pinch cayenne pepper

SERVES FOUR

1 Halve the avocados, remove the stones, then peel. Slice and brush with lemon juice, then arrange the slices on 4 plates.

2 Mix sauce ingredients together in a bowl, then fold in crab meat. Divide crab meat between plates and serve.

VARIATION Add toasted almonds, cashew nuts or unsalted peanuts to crab mixture in Step 2. If liked, serve the salad on a bed of salad leaves with a selection of warm crusty bread rolls.

SALAD NICOISE

Tuna, beans, hard-boiled eggs and anchovies tossed in French dressing.

125g (4oz) thin green beans, trimmed
6 tomatoes, quartered
½ cucumber, peeled and thinly sliced
1 red pepper, seeded and sliced
6 spring onions, sliced diagonally
200g (7oz) can tuna steak in oil, drained and flaked
90g (3oz) black olives, stoned
3 hard-boiled eggs, quartered
1tbsp chopped parsley
50g (1¾oz) can anchovies, drained

DRESSING
60ml (2fl oz) olive oil
1tbsp red wine vinegar
1tbsp lemon juice
¼tsp French mustard
salt and pepper

SERVES FOUR

1 Cook beans in a saucepan of boiling water for 4–5 minutes until just tender. Drain, rinse under cold water, then cut into 5cm (2in) lengths.

2 Put beans into a bowl with tomatoes, cucumber, red pepper, spring onions, tuna, olives and eggs.

3 Mix dressing ingredients together in a bowl, add to salad with parsley and toss gently.

4 Cut anchovy fillets in half lengthwise and arrange on top of salad.

> **VARIATION** Although this is a classic combination of ingredients, you may like to replace the tuna with sardines, or omit the anchovies.

46

TUNA & BEAN SALAD

This classic Italian salad makes a quick and easy supper served with crusty bread and a green salad.

470g (15oz) can cannellini or borlotti beans, drained
440g (14oz) can flageolet or haricot beans, drained
½ red onion, sliced
salt and pepper
2 × 200g (7oz) cans tuna steak in oil, drained and flaked
2tbsp chopped parsley

DRESSING
75ml (2½fl oz) olive oil
1tbsp red wine vinegar

SERVES FOUR

1 Put beans into a bowl with onion and salt and pepper. Add tuna fish and parsley.

2 Mix dressing ingredients together, then toss into salad.

> **VARIATION** Replace the cannellini and flageolet beans with other canned beans of your choice such as red kidney beans, butter beans, black-eyed beans or soya beans.

INDEX

Anchovies:
Anchovy Beignets 13
Anchovy & Pepper Gratin 25
Anchovy & Pepper Twists 9
Anchovy Toasts 15
Cheesy Anchovy Crêpes 30
Pissaladière 39
Salad Niçoise 46

Basic Crêpes 27

Cheesy Anchovy Crêpes 30
Cheesy Sardine Snacks 36

Crab:
Crab & Avocado Salad 45
Crab & Mackerel Salad 42
Crab Meat & Noodles 20
Devilled Crab Quiche 35
Seafood Crêpes 34

Deep Pan Pizza Dough 27
Devilled Crab Quiche 35

Fisherman's Pie 18

Herrings:
Spicy Herrings 26

Kippers:
Kipper & Lemon Pâté 14

Mackerel:
Crab & Mackerel Salad 42
Mackerel & Egg Crêpes 32

Mackerel & Tomato Crêpes 32
Savoury Crumble 22
Seafood Lasagne 17
Smokey Mackerel Mousse 6
Smoked Mackerel Salad 41

Midweek Pilchard Bake 18

Oriental Omelette 28

Pasta & Prawn Salad 44

Pilchards:
Midweek Pilchard Bake 18
Spicy Pilchard Treats 36

Pissaladière 39

Prawn:
Oriental Omelette 28
Pasta & Prawn Salad 44
Prawn & Almond Soup 8
Prawn & Pepper Crêpes 28
Prawn & Tuna Crêpes 31
Seafood Crêpes 34
Seafood Lasagne 17
Tuna & Prawn Pâté 16

Salad Niçoise 46

Salmon:
Salmon & Avocado Mousse 10
Salmon Mousse 10
Salmon Salad Pockets 36

Sardines:
Cheesy Sardine Snacks 36
Sardine Cobbler 22
Sardine & Tomato Pizza 40

Savoury Crumble 22
Seafood Crêpes 34
Seafood Lasagne 17

Sild:
Sild & Gerkin Slices 36

Skippers:
Skipper Poachies 36

Smoked Mackerel:
Crab & Mackerel Salad 42
Smokey Mackerel Mousse 6
Smoked Mackerel Salad 41

Spicy Herrings 26
Spicy Pilchard Treats 36

Traditional Pizza Dough 27

Tuna:
Fisherman's Pie 18
Prawn & Tuna Crêpes 31
Salad Niçoise 46
Tuna Bake 21
Tuna & Basil Tomatoes 12
Tuna & Bean Salad 46
Tuna & Onion Pizza 38
Tuna & Horseradish Sandwiches 36
Tuna & Macaroni Layer 24
Tuna & Prawn Pâté 16